The Shack that Dad Built

For my grandchildren—ER

Little Hare Books
4/21 Mary Street, Surry Hills
NSW 2010 AUSTRALIA

www.littleharebooks.com

First published 2004
First published in paperback 2005

National Library of Australia Cataloguing-in-Publication entry
Russell, Elaine 1941- .
The shack that dad built.

For children.
ISBN 1 877003 48 4 (hbk).
ISBN 1 877003 94 8 (pbk).

1. Aboriginal Australians – New South Wales – Sydney –
Juvenile fiction. I. Title

A823.4

Designed by ANTART
Printed in China
Produced by Phoenix Offset

2 4 5 3 1

Elaine Russell

The Shack that Dad Built

LITTLE  HARE

When I was Little

I was born in Tingha, in northern New South Wales, and when I was little we lived in Stony Gully. There was Mum, Dad, my big sister Violet, my big brothers Fred and Mervyn, me and my little sister Gloria.

Moving to Sydney

When I was about five we moved to Sydney
because my father, Clem, had found a job.
We went to live in La Perouse.

Some of Dad's cousins already lived there, and so did lots of
other Aborigines—some in the mission, some in shacks.
Dad didn't want to live in the mission, though.
He preferred to be independent.

The Shack that Dad Built

Dad decided to build a shack for us.
He chose a spot close to the beach with
a beautiful view across the bay.

The shack was made of bits of tin from
rubbish tips and had a dirt floor.
It was hot in summer and cold in winter,
but to us it was great.

Our New Home

We only had one big room in our shack. The walls were lined
with newspaper to help keep out the cold and heat. At night,
us kids would all sleep on a big mattress on the floor, the girls
up one end and the boys down the other.

During the day we would put the mattress away, and Violet and
I would sweep the floor. I sprinkled water on the dirt
so it didn't fly everywhere. Then Mum would put down an
old piece of lino. I thought it looked lovely!

The Biggest Backyard in the World

I thought my backyard was the biggest in the whole world!
We had the ocean and sand dunes and lots of bush where
lantana grew. We made tunnels through the lantana, and played
hide-and-seek in the bush and among the dunes.

Sometimes we played till it was nearly dark, even though we knew Dad was very strict. He warned us that if we didn't get home before the sun went down, the Little Hairy Men would get us. The bush at night could be a very scary place, with lots of strange noises. We were all frightened of the Little Hairy Men!

Bush Tucker

There were enormous Moreton Bay fig trees right near the mission.
We used to wait till the ripe fruit fell to the ground so
we could eat it. We also picked berries.

One day my father showed us a plant called Warrigal Greens
that was growing wild all around us. We picked bunches of it
and took it home to Mum. She boiled it up and it tasted just
like spinach. Our shack didn't have a kitchen, so Mum
did all the cooking outside over an open fire.

Fish for Supper

Living on the coast meant that a lot of our meals came from the sea. Whenever Mum went fishing on the rocks I wanted to go with her. While she fished, I'd prise oysters off the rocks and put them in an old tin. It wasn't easy—sometimes they stuck to the rocks very hard! When we got home, Mum would cook up a fish and oyster curry, which we'd eat with damper.

The other way to get fish was from the fishermen. We'd wait patiently as they pulled in their nets. When the nets were on the beach, the fish would jump out onto the sand, and kids ran from everywhere to try to grab them. I tried, but they were too slippery. Luckily, Fred and Mervyn could grab a lot between them. We always enjoyed supper on those nights!

My School

My sister Violet walked me to school on my first day, saying
"Hurry up! We'll be late!" When we got to the school gate, she
just left me there—she went to a different building
because she was older. I was scared!

I felt a lot better when we lined up to go to our classes.
I soon made some new friends and we played games in
the schoolyard. The next day I wasn't scared at all.

Money for Hot Chips

On the weekends, when the tourists came out to La Perouse,
they'd usually make their way down to the wharf.
There they'd throw coins into the sea and watch the kids dive
for them. I was too small to dive, so I would sit on the wharf
and hold the coins that my brothers collected.
Afterwards, we'd go and buy the biggest bag of hot chips we
could get, then sit on the beach and have a good feed.
Yum!

The golf course provided the local kids with another way to make money. Golfers often lost their balls in the long grass and bush around the course. Kids would watch where the balls went then come back later to find them. They'd take them home, give them a wash, and sell them back to the golfers— who were usually happy to get their favourite balls back!

My Secret Garden

No one in the world knew that I had my own secret garden. I didn't even tell my brothers and sisters—it was a special place just for me. It was hidden in a sand dune, and I only went there when no one was looking. I would collect wildflowers and shells from the beach then arrange them in a pretty pattern, which I covered with a flat piece of glass for protection.

Lantana grew everywhere around La Perouse in those days.
It had such beautiful little coloured flowers I had no idea it
was a weed! My friends and I picked hundreds of the
flowers and made garlands to put around our necks.
They made us feel beautiful.

The Hand of Friendship

One day, while we were playing outside our shack, we were surprised to see a family of gypsies coming down the road in a caravan pulled by a horse. They really seemed like strangers in a strange land. But my father extended the hand of friendship.

The gypsy family said we were the first people to make them
feel welcome. That night we all sat around a big campfire
telling our stories to each other.

My Saddest Christmas

One Christmas Eve, my parents took me and my brothers and
sisters to nearby Matraville, where a charity was giving away
toys to Aboriginal children. It was a very hot day,
and the queue was so long.

I watched lots of kids going home, happy with their dolls and bikes and scooters and toy cars. My heart was set on a doll that said "Mama, Mama". When we finally reached the head of the queue, the people told my parents that they'd run out of toys. I cried and cried.

From the Beach to the Bush

We used to sit around the campfire at night, and Dad would tell us about how he travelled all over the place before he and Mum started a family. Sometimes he'd tell us scary ghost stories. But one night, when I was about ten, he told us that we were going on a long trip. He had got a job as a handyman on a mission called Murrin Bridge, way out in the country. We would live in a house with floorboards and proper windows.

Not long after that, we packed up our clothes (there weren't many!) and said goodbye to our friends and to Violet, who was staying behind. We were all excited, but also sad at the thought of leaving La Perouse and the beach where we loved to swim and fish.

Leaving

Our journey began when we caught the tram from La Perouse
to Central Station. I forgot all about being sad when I saw
the big steam train that would take us to our new home.

I remember the train click-clacking out of Sydney and into
the bush. I looked out the window and saw thousands
of buttercups, like a big yellow carpet. It was such a
beautiful sight to see. I couldn't wait to get to our new home.

Sometimes I wonder what happened to the shack that Dad built.

Aboriginal people have lived on the east coast of Australia for more than 40 000 years, and La Perouse, on the shores of Botany Bay, has been used as a camping ground or meeting place for at least 7500 years. People followed the seasonal fishing between La Perouse and the south coast of New South Wales.

Records of permanent Aboriginal habitation at La Perouse date back to around 1880, when twenty-six Aborigines from the south coast took up permanent settlement. In the mid 1880s, the camp was officially established as an Aboriginal reserve. The camp was first run by missionaries and a policeman, and in later years by resident managers. Tin houses were built and, in 1894, a mission church. But the sand dunes they stood on were too unstable, and the mission buildings were moved to higher ground in 1929-1930.

These were the Depression years, and hundreds of unemployed people—black and white—moved into the area around the mission and set up camp, building shacks out of whatever materials they could find. As the Depression eased, many of the white people moved on, and by the time Elaine Russell and her family moved to La Perouse, the area was predominantly Aboriginal once more.

Fred, Violet, Mervyn
Elaine and Gloria